AF229632

Disclaimer

Table of Contents

Contents

Introduction

Ever since the 1980s, wrestling figures have ruled the minds and hearts of kids and tweens everywhere. It all started in the 80s with companies such as Mattel, Hasbro, and LJN fighting for market share.

The companies partnered with or were supported by shows that served as an advertisement medium for their licensed merchandise. Going with the trend at the time, LJN also entered into a partnership with the World Wrestling Federation (WWF), now known as World Wrestling Entertainment or WWE.

WWE is an entertainment and media group that organizes and promotes wrestling events. LJN's partnership with WWF gave the world some of the most legendary wrestling figures in history. 8-inch, heavy-duty rubber figures, the WWF LJN figures could withstand the most aggressive imaginary play.

This quality of the LJN figures was one of the main reasons they went onto become the most successful wrestling figures of the 1980s. However, what most people don't know is that the 8-inch, heavy-duty rubber figures of LJN were devised by accident.

The company had originally planned to build 3.75-inch wrestling figures, which was the standard for action figures at the time. However, the prototypes they sent to WWF for approval were the larger, 8-inch figures. Vince McMahon, the CEO and founder of the WWF, took an instant liking to these figures and suggested that LJN produce these instead of the 3.75-inch figures originally proposed.

McMahon felt that the 8-inch figures will do justice with the real-life wrestlers they represent. He insisted that the figures stay the size of the prototype and that is exactly what happened. This turned out to be a good decision not just for LJN and WWF, but also for the kids and tweens who would spend hours and hours recreating the scenes of their favorite fights.

As most people would already know, the LJN actions figures including the LJN wrestling superstar figures, LJN bendies figures, and LJN thumb wrestler figures became instant hits with the buyers of action figures. Even today, we don't find wrestling figures that have the same legendary status as the ones LJN made of Andre the Giant, Hulk Hogan, and the Ultimate Warrior.

In this price guide, we name our picks for the best wrestling figures among the LJN wrestling superstar figures, LJN bendies figures, and LJN thumb wrestler figures. We will also provide you with the best available prices for all LJN figures.

We believe that it can be hard for most people to track the value of LJN wrestling figures as there is no official price guide bible. However, after you've read this book or wrestling price guide, you'll know what LJN wrestling collectibles are available and what their price is. This will ensure that you don't buy a wrestling collectible for more than what it's worth. Additionally, this will help you to get the best possible deal for a collectible you own.

LJN Wrestling Superstar Figures

The 70s was an era that was ruled by small action figures that resembled the characters of the Star Wars and G.I. Joe. However, the 80s was all about wrestling figures, LJN wrestling figures to be more specific.

These 8-inch, heavy-duty rubber figures were almost twice the size of the highly sought-after small action figures of the 70s. Unlike most of the action figures from the 70s, the LJN wrestling figures did not come with a whole host of accessories. Instead, most of them include only a hat or cane.

In a way, the LJN figures were 'inaction figures' yet they were more popular than any figures before or after them. The most prized asset among boys in the 80s, the LJN wrestling figures are highly valued collectibles for today's grown adults.

While wrestling was watched by people across the U.S before this time, it was in the 80s that the sport really kicked off in the country. This was all thanks to the introduction of the WWF and the advent of wrestling figures such as the LJN wrestling superstars. These were the two main reasons for the surge in popularity of pro-wrestling in the 80s.

80s kids will rememberwhat the LJN wrestling figures meant to the fans of the World Wrestling Federation (WWF) at that time. The fans, especially young kids, would watch the televised fights of the WWF and then recreate the fight scenes using their LJN figures.

LJN was contracted in 1984 by Titan Sports, the owner of the WWF, to produce the first ever pro-wrestling figures. These figures were a toy representation of the real-life WWF superstars such as the Hulk Hogan and Andre the Giant.

The figures were made out of solid rubber and they were an instant hit with the kids and even some adults. Seeing the growing popularity of these figures, LJN started to produce wrestling figures one after the other. Many of these figures are a collector's gold today.

The reason for the massive popularity of the LJN figures in the 80s was that the kids of the time saw these figures as much more than action figures to play with. For many kids, these figures were a representation of their role models. Therefore, it wouldn't be farfetched to say that the LJN wrestling figures have played a role in shaping the personality of people who grew up in the 80s.

The LJN wrestling figures produced in the 80s were the LJN wrestling superstar figures. The company also produced bendies and thumb wrestler figures to go along with the wrestling superstar figures. However, it was the 8-inch LJN wrestling superstar figures that made their way into the heart of the 80s kids. Following are the 13 LJN wrestling superstar figures that almost every kid in the 80s wanted.

Hulk Hogan

Hulk Hogan is perhaps one of the most iconic wrestlers in the history of World Wrestling Entertainment (WWE). One of the biggest stars in the business, Hulk Hogan was the most sought-after LJN wrestling superstar figures by kids in the 80s. A favorite of many kids on the 80s, the Hulk Hogan figure is one a prized collectible today.

Whether it was the series 1 figure, the 15" figure, or a bendie, LJN's Hulk Hogan figure was loved by kids of all ages during the 80s. Currently, the price of the LJN Hogan figure varies based on the design, series, and size of the figure.

The current value of Hulk Hogan series 1 figure with no shirt is $50. The 15" is valued at $200. The prices of the Hulk Hogan Series 5 figures are considerably high. The Series 5 Hulk Hogan figure with the white shirt is valued at $335 while the Hulk Hogan figure with the red shirt is available for $375.

Keep in mind that carded figures which are figures that are in the original packaging can be valued at 100's or 1000's of dollars more. Depending on the condition of the packaging and the amount a collector is willing to pay, any carded figure can reach 100's or 1000's of dollars.

Andre the Giant

No LJN Wrestling Superstars collection would incomplete without the toy figure of Andre the Giant. The figure is not an exact representation of the real wrestler, as it seems to be in better shape than the real-life Andre the Giant. The figure comes without the bloated arms and fat that is found on the real-life Andre the Giant.

However, this description only applies to the Andre the Giant figure with short hair. There are other versions of the figure as well that do a better job of depicting the real-life Andre the Giant.

At present, the Andre the Giant series 3 figure is valued at $75. The Andre the Giant series 1 figure with long hair is currently priced at $60 and if you're a fan of the series 6 Andre the Giant figure with a black suit, then you can get it for $240.

Rowdy Roddy Piper

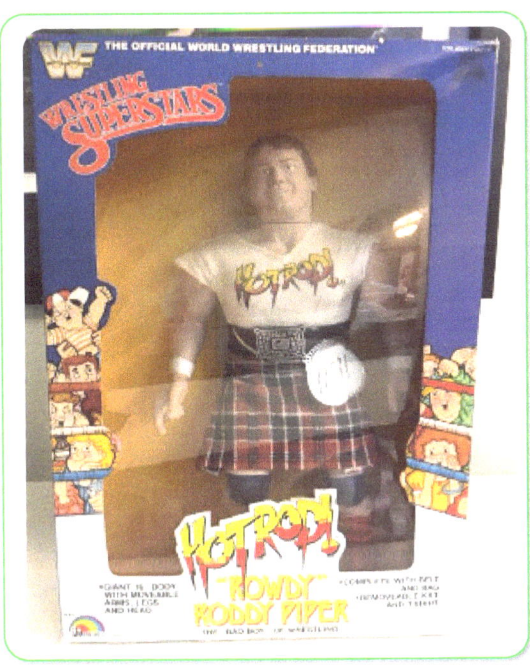

One of the first WWF figures produced by LJN, Rowdy Roddy Piper has been on the forefront of wrestling memorabilia. The Rowdy Roddy Piper LJN figure is a representation of a beloved member of the WWE Hall of Fame. Rowdy Roddy Piper could not be intimidated by anyone. This is exactly what LJN had in mind when it designed the Rowdy Roddy Piper.

As for the current value of the figure, the LJN series 1 Rowdy Roddy Piper is valued at $52. On the other hand, the LJN 15' figure of Rowdy Roddy Piper will cost you $165. If you were a fan of Rowdy Roddy Piper, then paying this amount for the figure would be worth it.

Adrian Adonis

Adrian Adonis wasn't part of the first three-figure series released by LJN. The first and only LJN Adrian Adonis figure was part of series 4. Despite this, Adrian Adonis was a famed figure during the 80s. An 8" figure of Adrian Adonis was a favorite of quite a few kids. However, there were many kids who wanted to stay far away from this 'strange looking' doll. This is one of the few reasons why the series 4 Adrian Adonis figure is currently valued at only $35.

The Iron Sheik figure was one of the first LJN figures launched as part of the 1984 LJN series 1. A representation of the former WWE champion Iron Sheik, this LJN figure was often bought to recreate some of the wrestler's most famous and nationalistic rivalries.

As for the current value of the Iron Shcik LJN figure, the Series 1 figure is priced at $30. Additionally, it is available as part of the tag team sets. The Iron Sheik tag team set which features the Nikolai Volkoff figure is priced at $125.

Randy Savage

Whether you grew up in the 80s, the 90s or even the 2000s, you can't be a true pro-wrestling fan unless you know about Randy Savage. Only a few, if any, wrestlers commanded the same stature in their prime as 'Macho Man' Randy Savage. For many years, Randy Savage was a people's favorite. The popularity of Randy Savage encouraged LJN to produce a figure in his likeness.

The Randy Savage wrestling figure was released as part of the LJN series 3 figures. The Randy Savage wrestling figure was part of most kids' wrestling figure collections. Today, you can get this figure for $40.

Special Delivery Jones

Although he wasn't as famous as the wrestlers mentioned above, Special Delivery or S.D Jones had a significant fanbase. He was the underdog that many wrestling fans wanted to see become a top dog. Unfortunately for them, that did not happen. Nevertheless, Special Delivery Jones is still remembered by the kids of 80s, especially those who played with the Special Delivery Jones figure.

An underdog championed by young fans, the Special Delivery Jones figure fought many fake fights and won almost all of them. The Special Delivery Jones figure was released for the first time as part of the LJN series 2 figures. The first S.D Jones figure to be released was the red variant. Today, the figure is valued at $30. The second and final Special Delivery Jones figure released by LJN was the series 3 S.D Jones figure with the yellow shirt. Today, you can buy this figure for $40.

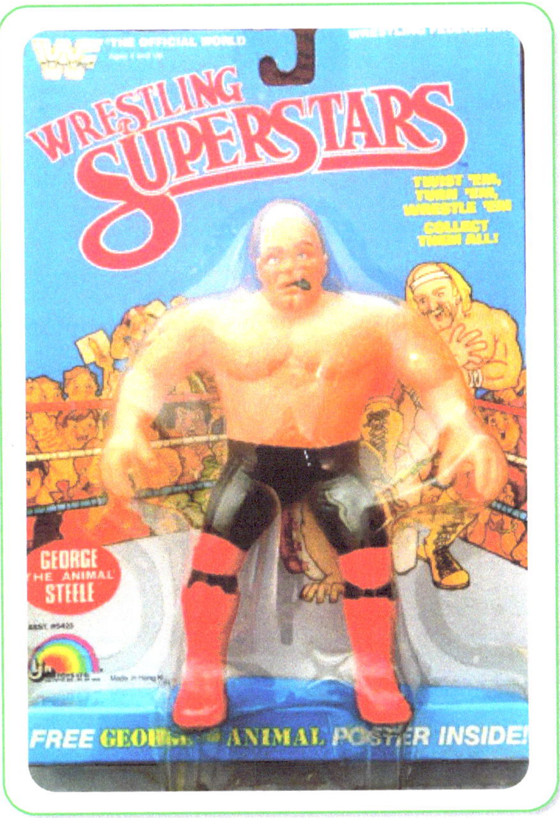

The LJN figure for George "The Animal" Steele is a toy representation of the most influential WWE wrestlers ever. The figure is a true representation of the real-life wrestlers, as it resembles a bald, hairy brute. Additionally, the figure looks as savage as the real-life George "The Animal" Steele. The LJN Wrestling Superstar figure also has the trademark green tongue and hairy torso of the real-life George the

Animal Steele. All in all, the LJN figure is as close to the real-life character as it could be.

As for the current value of the figure, the series 2 George "The Animal" Steele LJN figure is priced at $30. However, the figure is not part of any other LJN series launched in the 80s. While the figure is currently valued at $30, you may get it for a lower or higher price depending on the seller.

Honky Tonk Man

The Elvis impersonator of the WWF, Honky Tonk Man. It wouldn't be wrong to say that Honky Tonk Man added glamour to the WWF. As far as his wrestling abilities are concerned, he wasn't much to note about. He lost most of his matches, as he was usually 'outwrestled' by his opponents.

The Honky Tonk Man holds the longest reign as the Intercontinental Champion at 454 days but was almost always outwrestled. To win a majority of his matches, Honky Tonk Man would resort to despicable tactics or outside-the-ring interference.

Nevertheless, he was a fascinating character, and this was what propelled LJN to produce his figure as part of its series 6 figures. The current value of the Honky Tonk Man figure is $225.

The Ultimate Warrior

The Ultimate Warrior figure which was part of the series 6 LJN superstar figures is a toy representation of the famous wrestler who debuted in the WWE in 1987. Soon after making his debut, the Ultimate Warrior became an instant hit with the WWE fans and this created a demand for the Ultimate Warrior LJN figure.

Like the real-life Ultimate Warrior, the LJN figure representation
of the wrestler also had his face hidden under a painted mask.
Additionally, it comes with all the colorful attire that the WWE
superstar used to don.

As for as the current value of the LJN Ultimate Wrestling Superstar
figure, you can get the Series 6 LJN Ultimate Warrior figure for
about $450. However, you may be able to get a lower price by
bargaining with the seller.

Bret Hart

Released for the first time in 1987 as part of the LJN Wrestling
Superstars series 4, Bret 'The Hitman' Hart was a figure that became
an instant hit with the kids of the 80s. The figure pays homage to one
of the biggest superstars the world of wrestling has ever seen.

Bret Hart is reverently described as the 'Excellence of Execution'. Arguably the greatest technical wrestler in the history of WWE, Bret Hart was famous for his 'sharpshooter', a wrestling technique that siblings across thc United States would practice on each other

Additionally, the Bret 'The Hitman' Hart figure would be pit against figures of his WWF opponents and then the 'sharpshooter' would be practiced on them. Just like the real-life wrestler, the Bret 'The Hitman' Hart Wrestling Superstar figure is clad in black and pink tights. The figure also features the trademark Bret Hart boots and glasses. Bret Hart was the innovator of offense and he possessed an uncanny ability to create pinning combinations out of seemingly any predicament. The LJN Wrestling Superstar figure of Bret Hart allows you to recreate the action sequences of the wrestler.

As for the price or current value of the LJN Bret Hart Wrestling Superstar figure, you can get the figure for about $375. However, the figure might be available for less if you search all around.

Haku

Released in 1989, the LJN Haku Wrestling Superstar figure was part of the LJN Wrestling Superstar Series 6. The figure is a toy representation of the WWF wrestling superstar who was known for his toughness and the ability to intimidate.

Hailing from South Pacific Island of Tonga, Haku became a fearsome force in both the WWF and WCW in the 1980s and 1990s due to his unbridled intensity and brutal attacks. The Wrestling Superstar figure of Haku has been designed keeping all the characteristics of the real-life wrestler in mind.

Popularly known as King Tonga, Haku sported a beard and wore colorful tights and white bands on his wrists and ankles. The Haku LJN Wrestling Superstar figure has been designed with these exact same features or characteristics. As for the current value of the Haku LJN Wrestling Superstar figure, you can get the figure for $90.00. However, the price may be higher or lower depending on the availability of the wrestling figure.

Warlord

Released in 1989, the Warlord LJN Wrestling Superstar figure was part of the Series 6 LJN Wrestling Superstar figures just like the Haku LJN Wrestling Superstar figures. The figure is a toy representation of the WWF wrestling superstar who was often announced as 'Bigger than U.S Steel and more powerful than the Bilderberg group'.

The Warlord was the most physically imposing wrestler at a time when nearly every wrestler was physically imposing. This should be enough to give you an idea of the strength and caliber of the wrestler. The Warlord LJN Wrestling Superstar figure does justice to the real-life wrestler by depicting the physical strength and prowess of the wrestler.

The Warlord would often tag team with Ivan Koloff and The Barbarian to fight his wrestling adversaries who would be intimidated by the 6-foot-5 brute. Just like the real-life wrestler, the Warlord LJN Wrestling Superstar figure is designed to intimidate. Kids in the 80 and 90s would often turn to the Warlord figure when they needed an intimidating character to play with.

The Warlord LJN Wrestling Superstar figure dons the boots, wrist bands, and mask that were a regular feature on the real-life wrestler. As for the current value of the Warlord LJN Wrestling Superstar figure, you can get the figure for $85. However, just like the Haku Wrestling Superstar figure, the Warlord Wrestling Superstar figure may be priced higher or lower price depending on availability.

Big Boss Man

Released in 1989, the Big Boss Man LJN Wrestling Superstar figure was part of the Series 6 LJN Wrestling Superstar figures just like the Haku and Warlord LJN Wrestling Superstar figures. The figure is a toy representation of the one wrestling superstar who was entrusted with enforcing law, order, and justice in WWE.

A towering cop, the Big Boss Man made sure that anyone who dared to step up got served some hard time. This ruthless character of the real-life wrestler was kept in mind when designing the Big Boss Man LJN Wrestling Superstar figure.

A 300-plus pounder, the Big Boss Man muscled his foes the way he would subdue an unruly prisoner before handcuffing them to the ropes and introducing them to the business end of his trusty nightstick.

Although he was often brutal towards his foes, the Big Boss Man had morals. This was seen when the Million Dollar Man tried to buy his services. Instead of agreeing to work with Million Dollar Man, he let the wrestler know that he didn't come with a price tag. This defiance of the Big Boss Man endeared him to the WWE universe, making him one of the most popular wrestling superstars of the era.

All these qualities of the Big Boss Man were kept in mind when designing the Big Boss Man LJN Wrestling Superstar figure. The physical outlook of the wrestler was also kept in mind when designing the Big Boss Man wrestling figure. Just like the real-life wrestler, the toy figure dons a policeman uniform comprising of a blue half-sleeved shirt, a black pant, a belt, boots, and sunglasses.

As for the current value of the Big Boss Man Wrestling Superstar figure, you can get the figure for $90. However, just like the Haku and Warlord Wrestling Superstar figures, the Big Boss Man Wrestling Superstar figure may be priced higher or lower price depending on availability,

condition, and whether the figure is carded with the original packaging or not.

Sargent Slaughter Mail Away Figure

Although the figure was not designed by LJN, the Sargent Slaughter Mail Away figure was one of the most prized wrestling figures of the late 80s. Thus, we had to include it here as a bonus figure.

Manufactured by Hasbro, the Sargent Slaughter Mail Away figure was an 8-inch wrestling figure. The figure was a toy representation of one of the most recognizable WWE wrestlers ever. An icon to many American kids in the 80s and 90s, Sgt. Slaughter was a U.S marine turned wrestling superstar.

After proudly serving his country, Sargent Slaughter burst onto the wrestling scene in 1974 with a stint with the American Wrestling Association (AWA). He started his wrestling career under his real name Robert Remus.

Trained by WWE Hall of Famer Verne Gagne, Sargent Slaughter donned a mask and debuted in the WWE in 1980 as the brutal bullying drill instructor. The wrestler would often send fear down the spine of his opponents. Less than one year on, Sargent Slaughter was fighting with wrestling legends such as Andre the Giant, Pat Patterson, Pedro Morales, and Bruno Sammartino.

Like the real-life wrestler, the Hasbro Sargent Slaughter Mail Away figure dons a sleeveless green colored t-shirt, black tights, boots, gloves, and red wristbands. The idea was to make the figure as real as possible.

In addition to the same clothing as a real-life wrestler, the Hasbro Sargent Slaughter Mail Away figure also has the physical resemblance of the real-life Sargent Slaughter. This is the reason you find muscles on the Sargent Slaughter Hasbro figure.

As for the current value of the Hasbro Sargent Slaughter Mail Away figure, you can get the figure for $250. However, the Hasbro Sargent Slaughter Mail Away figure may be priced higher or lower price depending on availability.

There you have it—fifteen of the very best LJN Wrestling Superstar figures. If you currently own any of the above-mentioned figures, then you stand to earn a fortune. To help you find out the worth of your 80's LJN figure, we are going to provide a complete list of the LJN Wrestling Superstar figures with their prices at the end of this price guide.

LJN Wrestling Superstars Tag Team Boxed Sets

The LJN also offered the Tag Team Box sets. Each Tag Team box set came with a poster and two brown bag champion's belts. However, Strike Force came with black belts. Following are these Tag Team Box sets with their current value.

Tag Team Box Set	Price
The Hart Foundation: Bret Hart & Jim Neidhart	$450.00+
British Bulldogs: Davey Boy Smith & Dynamite Kid	$200.00+
Iron Sheik & Nikolai Volkoff	$100.00
The Killer Bee's Brian Blair & Jim Brunzell	$125.00
Hulk Hogan & Hillbilly Jim	$95.00
Greg Valentine & Brutus Beefcake	$85.00
Strike Force: Tito Santana & Rick Martel	$200.00

LJN Bendies Figures

Fashioned after the original 8-inch LJN Wrestling Superstar series, the LJN Bendies figures used the same paint scheme and pose as their taller version. The difference between the 8-inch Wrestling Superstar figures and the LJN Bendies figures was that the latter were much smaller in size. Additionally, they had metal wires inside which allowed the toys to bend.

Featuring unique molds, the LJN Bendies figures featured 18 figures in total and they have one major and several minor variations. The only major variant in the LJN Bendies figures is the Hulk Hogan which has blue knee pads instead of red and is taller than the rest of the line.

The mid-1980s was the time of the wrestling boom. This was the same time when the LJN Bendies figures were produced. The size of the LJN Bendies figures ranges between 4.25-inches and 4.75-inches. Most of the LJN Bendies figures are exact replicas of their LJN 8-inch counterparts. However, there are some exceptions.

To add to your knowledge, there are two variations on the packaging. The first release was on a card that resembled the package of the 8-inch LJN line, while the second release was on the card similar to those of the Rock 'n' Wrestling erasers.

On the first card, only a few of the bendies were released. There are also several figure variations in this line, which is what makes it so much fun. Four wrestlers in the LJN Bendies figures were produced both with and without laces on their boots. They include Orndorff, Sheik, Hogan, and Piper. The first releases are the ones without laces, while all releases after that had the laces.

In addition to the above, there is a third variation on Hulk Hogan. This variation is the blue kneepads version of the Hogan. The figure is a good .25-inch taller than the rest of the figures in the series. Because of this, the Hulk Hogan figure does not really fit in with the other figures in the LJN Bendies figures. The Hogan figure comes exclusively with the Bendie ring. However, that is not for certain.

When it comes to the ring, there are a few variations on it. There are two different colored cages: gray and a cream/fresh color. Additionally, there are two different colors of ring posts: red and blue. As for which versions are rare, no one is absolutely sure. He, we will briefly look at each of the LJN Bendies figures that were part of both the Single figures series and the tag team two-packs. We will discuss the physical characteristics of these figures as well as how much they cost. So, let's get started.

Single Figures

Following are the LJN Bendies figures that were part of the LJN Single Figures series. We will start with the Andre the Giant figure.

Andre the Giant

The Andre the Giant Bendies figure is a smaller version of the original Andre the Giant wrestling superstar figure. We have already gone into the details of the wrestler the toy figure represents. So, here we will talk only about the appearance of the figure.

Of course, the biggest distinction between the original Andre the Giant figures and the Bendies version is the size and the bendability of the figure. However, another noticeable difference is that the original Andre the Giant figure has long hair while the Bendies version comes with short hair.

As for the current value of the Andre the Giant Bendies figure, it is available at xxx. However, the price may vary depending on availability and other factors.

Big John Studd

The Big John Studd Bendies figure is the Bendies version of the Big John Studd figures that was launched as part of the Series 1 LJN Wrestling Superstar figures launched in 1984. The figure is a toy representation of the greatest Goliaths in WWE history Big John Studd.

Standing 6-foot-10 inches tall, Big John Studd weighed 354 pounds and was a mountain of a man who dominated his competition. The wrestler's rivalries with the Hulk Hogan and Andre the Giant are considered amongst the greatest in WWE history.

Like the Original Big John Studd Wrestling Superstar figure, the Bendies version also dons white tights and red boots. However, the Bendies version is a little leaner than the original Big John Studd figure.

As for the current value of the Big John Studd Bendies figure, it is priced at $16.00. However, the price can vary depending on availability, condition, and other factors.

King Kong Bundy

The King Kong Bundy Bendies figure is the Bendies version of the original King Kong Bundy figure that was released as part of the LJN series 2 Wrestling Superstar figures in 1985. Appearance-wise, the Bendies King Kong Bundy figure is exactly the same as the original version. It has the same body type and dons the same black costume and boots as the original King Kong Bundy.

Both the original and Bendies King Kong Bundy figures are toy representation of the 'earth-shaking' wrestler King Kong Bundy. Weighing a massive 458 pounds, King Kong Bundy used to stomp his way into WWE rings and he made an impact by destroying opponents with his Avalanche Splash and the demanding a five-count from the referee.

The highlight of the King Kong Bundy's career was his fight with Hulk Hogan in a steel cage for the WWE championship. For all these reasons, the LJN King Kong Bundy Bendies figure is a prized asset. The current value of the LJN King Kong Bundy Bendies figure is $16. However, the price can vary depending on availability, condition, and other factors.

Corporal Kirchner

The Corporal Kirchner Bendies figure is the Bendies version of the original Corporal Kirchner figure that was released as part the series 3 LJN Wrestling Superstar figures launched in 1986. There is no difference in the appearance of the Corporal Kirchner original Bendies versions. Both figures feature a green sleeveless shirt, commando-style pants, and a red cap.

The Corporal Kirchner Bendies figure is a toy representation of the WWE wrestler who's remembered as a patriot and an all-American good guy who defended his country's honor against loathed Russian Volkoff at WrestleMania 2.

Part of the 82nd Airborne Division, Kircher was a paratrooper who spent a good part of his teenage life leaping out of airplanes and training for intense combat situations. Although he never went into battle, Kirchner gained the mental and physical tenacity of a soldier. This was reflected in all his fights in WWE.

The patriotism reflected in the real-life Corporal Kirchner made the Corporal Kirchner figure a favorite of many people in the 80s. Today, the Bendies version of the figure is priced at $16. However, the price can vary depending on availability, condition, and other factors.

Jesse the Body Ventura

Jesse "The Body" Ventura Bendies figure is the Bendies version of the original Jesse Ventura figures that was released as part of the series 3 LJN Wrestling Superstar figures launched in 1986. There is no difference in the appearance of the Jesse Ventura original and Bendies versions. Both figures feature pink tights, light blue boots, and a light-blue head-gear.

The Jesse "The Body" Ventura figure is a toy representation of the colorful and influential WWE superstar Jesse Ventura. A Navy SEAL, a Vietnam Veteran, a ground-breaking television commentator, and the governor of Minnesota, Jesse Ventura was a larger-than-life wrestler.

As an in-ring superstar, Jesse Ventura is remembered for his legendary arm—The East-West Connection — with the late Adrian Adonis in the early 1980s. He is also remembered for his feuds with the likes of Tony Atlas, Ivan Putski, and WWE Champion Bob Backlund.

After retiring from wrestling, Jesse Ventura served as one of the most controversial announcers in WWE history. For these reasons and more, the Jesse Ventura figure is one of the most sought-after wrestling figures today.

The current value of the Jesse "The Body" Ventura Bendies figure is $16. However, the price may vary depending on availability, condition, and other factors.

Bobby Heenan

Bobby Heenan Bendies figure is the Bendies version of the original Bobby Heenan figure that was released as part of the series 3 LJN Wrestling Superstar figures in 1986. There is no difference in the appearance of the Bobby Heenan original and the Bendies version. Both figures feature a dark blue full-sleeve shirt with a BH logo, black pants, and black shoes.

The Bobby Heenan figures is a toy representation of the man who has been hailed by many as 'the brain' behind some of the most prolific superstars in WWE history. WWE superstars under Heenan's guidance came to be known as the Heenan Family.

Members of the Heenan Family included legends like Nick Bockwinkel, the Blackjacks, Big John Studd, King Kong Bundy, "Ravishing" Rick Rude, "Mr. Perfect" Curt Hennig, the Brain Busters, Harley Race, and the first WWE Hall of Famer, Andre the Giant.

The current value of the Bobby Heenan Bendies figures is $16. However, the price may vary depending on availability, condition, and other factors.

Brutus Beefcake

The Brutus Beefcake Bendies figure is the Bendies version of the original Brutus Beefcake figure that was released as part of the series 2 LJN Wrestling Superstar figures in 1985. There is no difference in the appearance of the Brutus Beefcake original and the Bendies version. Both figures feature pink tights, black boots, and black armbands.

The Brutus Beefcake figure is a toy representation of the famous WWE wrestler who was known as the flamboyant hairdresser who clipped the locks of WWE rivals. Often called Brutus "The Barber" Beefcake, the marquee superstar battled rivals like The Honky Tonk Man and Mr. Perfect and competed in main event matches alongside his good friend, Hulk Hogan, at SummerSlam '89 and WrestleMania IX. However, the greatest accomplishment of Brutus Beefcake was his defiant return to the ring in 1991 after a freak accident that nearly ended his life.

For all the above reasons, the Brutus Beefcake figure is highly sought-after by WWE fans worldwide. As for the current value of the figure, it is priced at $16. However, the price may vary depending on availability, condition, and other factors.

George Steele

The George Steele Bendies figure is the Bendies version of the original George Steel figure that was released as part of the series 2 LJN Wrestling Superstar figures in 1985. There is no difference in the appearance of the George Steele original and the Bendies version. Both figures sport a bald look and feature black tights and red boots.

As for the current value of the Brutus Beefcake Bendies figure, it is priced at $16. However, the price may vary depending on availability, condition, and other factors.

Hulk Hogan

The Hulk Hogan Bendies figure is the Bendies version of the original Hulk Hogan figure that was released as part of the series 1 LJN Wrestling Superstar figures in 1984. There is no difference in the appearance of the Hulk Hogan original and the Bendies version. Both figures sport blond hair and feature yellow shots, yellow boots, and wrist bands.

As for the current value of the Hulk Hogan Bendies figure, it is priced at $16. However, the price may vary depending on availability, condition, and other factors.

Iron Sheikh

The Iron Sheikh Bendies figure is the Bendies version of the original Iron Sheikh figure that was released as part of the series 1 LJN Wrestling Superstar figures in 1984. There is no difference in the appearance of the Iron Sheikh original and the Bendies version. Both figures sport blond hair and feature purple tights, and multi-colored boots.

As for the current value of the Hulk Hogan Bendies figure, it is priced at $16. However, the price may vary depending on availability, condition, and other factors.

Roddy Piper

The Roddy Piper Bendies figure is the Bendies version of the original Roddy Piper figure that was released as part of the series 1 LJN Wrestling Superstar figures in 1984. There is no difference in the appearance of the Roddy Piper original and the Bendies version. Both figures sport brown hair and feature red shorts with a belt, a white t-shirt with 'Hot Rod' written on it, and red boots. However, a variant of the Roddy Piper Bendies figure is also available.

As for the current value of the Roddy Piper Bendies figure, it is priced at $16. However, the price may vary depending on availability, condition, and other factors.

Nikolai Volkoff

The Nikolai Volkoff Bendies figure is the Bendies version of the original Nikolai Volkoff figure that was released as part of the series

1 LJN Wrestling Superstar figures in 1984. There is no difference in the appearance of the Nikolai Volkoff and the Bendies version. Both figures sport black hair and a French beard and feature a red costume and boots.

The Nikolai Volkoff figure is a toy representation of the WWE wrestler who stood the test of time. Best known as the evil Russian who teamed up with The Iron Sheik to become a World Tag Team Champion, Nikolai Volkoff was part of one of the most hated duos in WWE history.

The trademark of Volkoff was his insistence that the audience stands up out of respect as he would go on to deliver an ear-piercing rendition of the Soviet National Anthem. All this made him a highly hated but popular WWE wrestling superstar. This is the reason for the high demand of the Nikolai Volkoff figures both now and in the 80s.

As for the current value of the Nikolai Volkoff Bendies figure, it is priced at $16. However, the price may vary depending on availability, condition, and other factors.

Hillybilly Jim

The Hillybilly Jim Bendies figure is the Bendies version of the original Hillybilly Jim figure that was released as part of the series 1 LJN Wrestling Superstar figures in 1984. There is no difference in the appearance of the Hillybilly original and the Bendies version. Both figures sport long black hair and a beard and feature a blue dress with a red-colored sleeveless shirt underneath and black shoes.

The Hillybilly Jim figure is a toy representation of the WWE crowd favorite and fun-loving powerhouse from Mudlick, Ky Hillybilly

Jim. After being presented with his first pair of wrestling boots by
The Hulkster, Jim quickly transitioned from an overeager follower
to a bona fide sports-entertainer.

Sporting a shaggy beard, bib overalls, and a horseshoe-chain
necklace, Hillbilly Jim weighed 320 pounds and was 6-foot-7 inch
tall. This intimidated many WWE wrestlers of his time. At the same
time, it increased the appeal of the Hillybilly Jim figure.

As for the current value of the Roddy Piper Bendies figure, it
is priced at $16. However, the price may vary depending on
availability, condition, and other factors.

Randy Savage

The Randy Savage Bendies figure is the Bendies version of the
original Randy Savage figure that was released as part of the series
3 LJN Wrestling Superstar figures in 1986. There is no difference
in the appearance of the Randy Savage original and the Bendies
version. Both figures sport long hair and a beard and feature pink
shorts, yellow boots, a yellow headband, and sunglasses.

As for the current value of the Randy Savage figure, it is priced
at $16. However, the price may vary depending on availability,
condition, and other factors.

Junkyard Dog

Putting a Bendies spin on the original, The Junkyard Dog Bendies
figure was released as part of the Series 1 LJN Wrestling Superstars
figures in 1984. There is no difference in the appearance of the
Junkyard Dog original and the Bendies version. Both figures have
dilated pupils, red tights, and white boots.

As for the current value of the figure, it is priced at $16. However, the price may vary depending on availability, condition, and other factors.

Lou Albano

The Lou Albano Bendies figure is the Bendies version of the Lou Albano original figure that was released as part of the Series 3 LJN Wrestling Superstars figures in 1986. There is no difference in the appearance of the Lou Albano original and the Bendies version. Both figures sport a French beard and feature black tights, a white t-shirt with the wrestler's face imprinted on it, and a light blue overcoat and white-colored shoes.

As for the current value of the figure, it is priced at $16. However, the price may vary depending on availability, condition, and other figures.

Ricky Steamboat

The Ricky Steamboat Bendies figure is the Bendies version of the Ricky Steamboat original figure that was released as part of the Series 3 LJN Wrestling Superstars figure in 1986. There is no difference in the appearance of the Ricky Steamboat original and the Bendies version. Both figures have a muscular body and feature black tights and boots.

Paul Orndorff

The Paul Orndorff Bendies figure is the Bendies version of the Paul Orndorff original figure that was released as part of the Series 3 LJN Wrestling Superstars figure in 1986. There is no difference in the appearance of the Paul Orndorff original and the Bendies version. Both figures have a muscular body and feature red shorts and boots.

Tag Team Champions Two-Packs

The Tag Team Two-Packs comprised of six Tag Team packs.
Following is a brief introduction to each:

Captain Lou and George the Animal Steele

This Tag Team Champions set comprises of the Lou Albano
and George the Animal Steele LJN wrestling figures. The set is
currently priced at $50. However, the price may vary depending on
availability, condition, and other factors.

King Kong Bundy and Big John Studd

This Tag Team Champions set comprises of the King Kong
Bundy and Big John Studd LJN wrestling figures. The set is
currently priced at $50. However, the price may vary depending on
availability, condition, and other factors.

Hulk Hogan and Junkyard Dog

This Tag Team Champions set comprises of the Hulk Hogan and
Junkyard Dog LJN wrestling figures. The set is currently priced
at $50. However, the price may vary depending on availability,
condition, and other factors.

Iron Sheik and Nikolai Volkoff

This Tag Team Champions set comprises of the Iron Sheik and
Nikolai Volkoff LJN wrestling figures. The set is currently priced
at $50. However, the price may vary depending on availability,
condition, and other factors

Ricky Steamboat and Corporal Kirchner

This Tag Team Champions set comprises of the Ricky Steamboat and Corporal Kirchner LJN wrestling figures. The set is currently priced at $50. However, the price may vary depending on availability, condition, and other factors.

Jesse Ventura and Randy Savage

This Tag Team Champions set comprises of the Jesse Ventura and Randy Savage LJN wrestling figures. The set is currently priced at $50. However, the price may vary depending on availability, condition, and other factors.

The above are the tag team two-packs produced by LJN.

LJN Thumb Wrestlers

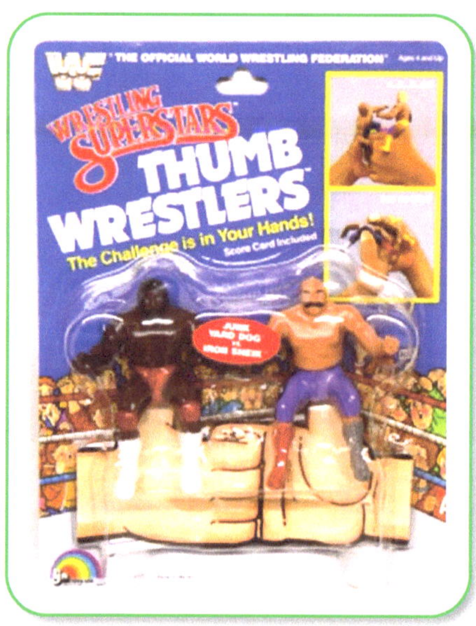

The LJN Thumb Wrestlers consisted of twelve LJN figures that were sold in two-packs. Compared to the other figures, Jake Roberts and King Kong Bundy were produced in very small quantities.

Conclusion

WWE is an entertainment and media group that organizes and promotes wrestling events. LJN's partnership with WWF gave the world some of the most legendary wrestling figures in history. 8-inch, heavy-duty rubber figures, the WWF LJN figures could withstand the most aggressive imaginary play.

In addition to the original 8-inch figures, LJN also produced Bendies version of these figures as well as Tag Team and Thumb Wrestler Sets.

Most people find it hard to track the value of the different LJN wrestling figures as there is no official price guide bible. However, this wrestling price guide allows you to know what LJN wrestling collectibles are available and what their price is.

Refer to the **bonus price list supplement below** to find how much your wrestling figure is worth or how much you'll need to pay to get that coveted wrestling figure!

The Price Guide

LJN Wrestling Superstars Series 1 1984	
Figure	**Price**
Andre The Giant: Long Hair	$60.00
Big John Studd	$42.00
Hillbilly Jim	$30.00
Hulk Hogan	$50.00
Iron Sheik	$30.00
Junk Yard Dog	$35.00
Jimmy "Superfly" Snuka	$65.00
Nikolai Volkoff	$35.00

LJN Wrestling Superstars Series 2 1985	
Figure	**Price**
Brutus Beefcake	$35.00
George "The Animal" Steele	$30.00
Greg "the Hammer" Valentine	$35.00
King Kong Bundy	$40.00
Paul "Mr. Wonderful" Orndorff	$35.00
Special Delivery Jones: Red Shirt	$30.00

LJN Wrestling Superstars 15' Figures 1985	
Figure	**Price**
Hulk Hogan	$100.00
"Rowdy" Roddy Piper	$165.00

LJN Wrestling Superstars Series 3	
Figure	**Price**
Andre the Giant: Short Hair	$75.00+
Bobby "the Brain" Heenan	$40.00
Bruno Sammartino	$40.00
Captain Lou Albano	$30.00
Corporal Kirchner	$30.00
The Magnificent Muraco	$35.00
Terry Funk	$45.00
Classie Freddie Blassie	$40.00
Jessie "The Body" Ventura	$150.00
Jimmy "Mouth of the South" Hart	$35.00
Randy "Macho Man" Savage	$40.00
Ricky "The Dragon" Steamboat	$35.00
SD Special Delivery Jones Yellow Shirt	$40.00
Tito Santana	$40.00

LJN Wrestling Superstars Series 4	
Figure	**Price**
Adrian Adonis	$35.00
Billy Jack Haynes	$55.00
Bret "Hitman" Hart	$375.00
B Brian Blair	$50.00
"Cowboy Boy" Bob Orton	$35.00
Elizabeth	$65.00
Hercules Hernandez	$45.00
Jake "The Snake" Roberts	$55.00
"Jumping" Jim Brunzell	$40.00
Jim "the Anvil "Neidhart	$325.00
Kamala	$70.00
King Harley Race	$260.00
Koko B. Ware	$125.00
Mean Gene	$35.00
Mr. Fuji	$35.00
Outback Jack	$50.00
Ted Arcidi	$40.00

LJN Wrestling Superstars Series 5	
Figure	**Price**
Ax of Demolition	$95.00
Bam Bam Bigelow	$90.00
Hacksaw Jim Duggan	$60.00
Hulk Hogan #2 White Shirt	$235.00
Hulk Hogan #3 Red Shirt	$275.00
Johnny Valiant	$35.00
Ken Patera	$60.00
One Man Gang	$70.00
Referee	$70.00
Slick	$30.00
Ric Martel	$100.00
"The Million Dollar Man" Ted Dibiase	$60.00
Vince McMahon	$40.00

LJN Wrestling Superstars Series 6	
Figure	**Price**
Andre the Giant	$140.00
Ax of Demolition	$95.00
Bam Bam Bigelow	$90.00
Big Boss Man	$90.00
Honky Tonk Man	$125.00
Hulk Hogan #4 White Shirt	$235.00
Hulk Hogan #5Red Shirt	$275.00
Haku	$90.00

"Ravishing" Rick Rude	$75.00
Ultimate Warrior	$450.00
Warlord	$85.00

Hasbro (LJN) Sargent Slaughter Mail Away Figure:	**250.00+**

LJN Wrestling Superstars Tag Team Champions Two-Packs	
Figure	**Price**
Hulk Hogan & Junkyard Dog	$50.00
The Iron Sheik & Nikolai Volkoff	$50.00
George Steele & Captain Lou Albano	$50.00
King Kong Bundy & Big John Studd	$50.00
Randy Savage & Jesse Ventura	$50.00
Ricky Steamboat & Corporal Kirchner	$50.00

LJN Wrestling Superstars Tag Team Box Set	Price
The Hart Foundation: Bret Hart & Jim Neidhart	$450.00+
British Bulldogs: Davey Boy Smith & Dynamite Kid	$200.00+
Iron Sheik & Nikolai Volkoff	$100.00
The Killer Bee's Brian Blair & Jim Brunzell	$125.00
Hulk Hogan & Hillbilly Jim	$95.00
Greg Valentine & Brutus Beefcake	$85.00
Strike Force: Tito Santana & Rick Martel	$200.00

LJN Bendies Single Figures	
Figure	**Price**
André the Giant	$16.00
Big John Studd	$16.00
Bobby Heenan	$16.00
Brutus Beefcake	$16.00
Captain Lou Albano	$16.00
Corporal Kirchner	$16.00
George "The Animal" Steele	$16.00
Hillbilly Jim	$16.00
Hulk Hogan (red or blue knee-pad versions)	$16.00
The Iron Sheik	$16.00
Jesse "The Body" Ventura	$16.00
Junkyard Dog	$16.00
King Kong Bundy	$16.00
"Mr. Wonderful" Paul Orndorff	$16.00
Nikolai Volkoff	$16.00
"Macho Man" Randy Savage	$16.00
Ricky "The Dragon" Steamboat	$16.00
"Rowdy" Roddy Piper	$16.00

LJN Thumb Wrestler Set (Two Packs Carded)	Price
Paul Orndorff and Roddy Piper	$200.00
Jake Roberts and Ricky Steamboat	$300.00
Paul Orndorff and King Kong Bundy (Rare)	$200.00
Hillbilly Jim and Randy Savage	$100.00
Hillybilly Jim and Roddy Piper	$100.00
Hulk Hogan and Iron Sheik	$90.00
Hulk Hogan and Big John Studd	$90.00
Hulk Hogan and Nikolai Volkoff	$90.00
Hulk Hogan and Roddy piper	$100.00
Junkyard Dog and Roddy Piper	$100.00
Junkyard Dog and Nikolai Volkoff	$90.00
Hulk Hogan and Randy Savage	$100.00

LJN Thumb Wrestler (Loose Figures)	Price
Hillbilly Jim	$15.00
Big John Studd	$15.00
Hulk Hogan	$15.00
Randy Savage	$20.00
Junk Yard Dog	$15.00
Rowdy Roddy Piper	$20.00
Iron Sheik	$15.00
Paul Orndorff	$15.00
Nikolai Volkoff	$15.00
Ricky Steamboat	$20.00
King Kong Bundy (Rare)	$75.00
Jake the Snake Roberts (Rare)	$100.00

VISIT US AT

www.wrestlingpriceguides.com